Beginner Bass Guitar Lessons Book

Includes Online Audio Access

by
Bert Casey

For Online Audio Access, go to this internet address:

cvls.com/extras/begbass

Introduction

The *Beginner Bass Guitar lessons* with Audio Access will quickly transform you from an absolute beginner into a student/bassist with a full understanding of the fundamentals and techniques of bass playing. This clear, step-by-step method includes many photographs, large easy-to-read notation and tablature, and a sequence of learning that has been meticulously developed and tested over a 20 year period. With each new song, you will learn new techniques to establish a firm foundation that will enable you to enjoy playing bass for many years.

The Author

Bert Casey, the author of this book, has been a professional performer and teacher in the Atlanta area for over 30 years. He plays several instruments (acoustic guitar, electric guitar, bass, mandolin, banjo, ukulele, and flute) and has written seven other courses (*Acoustic Guitar Primer, Acoustic Guitar Book 2, Electric Guitar Primer, Ukulele Primer, Mandolin Primer, Bluegrass Fakebook, & Flatpicking Guitar Song*s. Bert performed many years in Atlanta and the Southeast with his bands Home Remedy and Blue Moon. His talent and willingness to share have helped thousands of students learn and experience the joy of playing a musical instrument.

Watch & Learn Products Really Work

30 years ago, Watch & Learn revolutionized music instructional courses by developing well thought out, step-by-step instructional methods combined with clear, easy-to-understand graphics that were tested for effectiveness on beginners before publication. This concept, which has dramatically improved the understanding and success of beginning students, has evolved into the Watch & Learn mastermind of authors, editors, teachers, and artists that continue to set the standard of music instruction today. This has resulted in sales of almost 2 million products since 1979. This high quality course will significantly increase your success and enjoyment while playing the bass.

Audio Access

For Audio Access, go to this internet address:

cvls.com/extras/begbass

Table of Contents

Audio Tracks

The accompanying Audio Tracks contain all of the lessons in the book. Each lesson is recorded in its entirety. The songs are played twice, a slow version using only the bass, and an up tempo version using a full band (drums, guitar, bass, keyboard, and vocals). The music is mixed in stereo with the bass on the left channel and the other instruments on the right channel so that you can adjust the bass volume to suit your tastes. The Audio Tracks contains the following songs, which are recorded by permission:

Song 1 - Getting Started
Song 2 - Good Hearted Woman
Song 3 - Old Time Rock & Roll
Song 4 - That'll Be The Day
Song 5 - The Wanderer
Song 6 - Peaceful, Easy Feeling
Song 7 - Johnny B. Goode
Song 8 - 12 Bar Blues In E
Song 9 - Walking Eighths In A
Song 10 - Kansas City
Song 11 - Walking Up The Neck
Song 12 - Bass Runs In G
Song 13 - Walking Two Beat
Song 14 - Slow Rock
Song 15 - Rock Shuffle In D
Song 16 - Addicted To Love
Song 17 - Billy Jean
Song 18 - Under My Thumb
Song 19 - La Bamba

For Audio Access, go to this internet address:

cvls.com/extras/begbass

How to Use the Book & Audio Tracks

To use the book and audio together, follow these suggestions.

Step 1
Listen to a section of the audio. Rewind and listen again until you understand it completely.

Step 2
Once you understand the section, go to the book to practice the exercises and songs over and over until you are comfortable with them.

Step 3
After practicing with the book, go back and play along with the audio to make sure you are performing the material properly.

This course is designed to be worked through, stopping and practicing each section until you are thoroughly familiar with it. It will probably take the average beginning student 2 - 4 months to work all the way through the book and audio, so don't get in a hurry. Take your time and learn the material correctly.

Special Thanks To:

GEOFF HOHWALD
for help in writing this book

HOWARD CAREY
for playing keyboards on the Audio Tracks

Section 1
Getting Started

Parts of the Bass

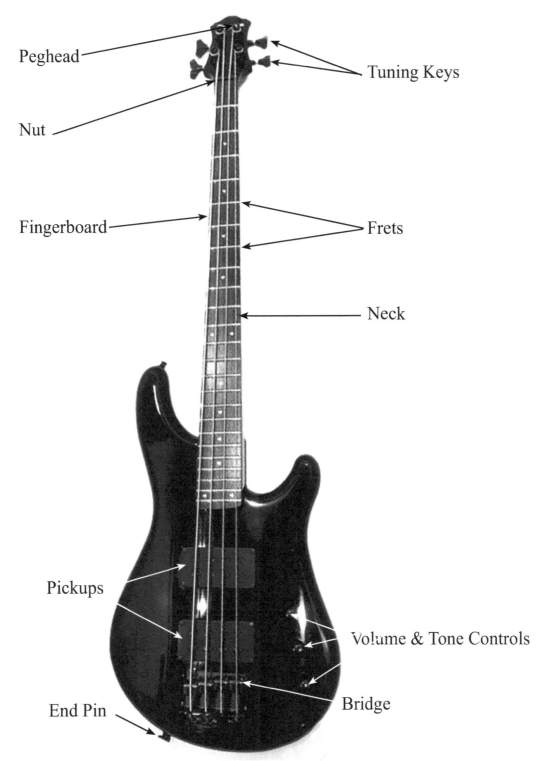

Peghead

Tuning Keys

Nut

Fingerboard

Frets

Neck

Pickups

Volume & Tone Controls

Bridge

End Pin

You will need a bass amplifier and a good cord. Make sure your amp is in good condition and doesn't produce any noise or hum. There are many combinations of wattage and speaker size in bass amps. Get one that you can afford and that sounds good. A nice feature is a head phone jack so you can practice without disturbing anyone. Buy a new cord so that you don't have to worry about noise problems from a bad cord.

Holding the Bass

At first you'll be playing the bass sitting down. Use a straight backed chair so that you can sit with good posture and have free arm movement without banging the bass or your arms on the furniture.

Sit erect with both feet on the floor and the bass resting on your right thigh. The bass should be braced against your stomach with the right forearm so that the neck of the bass doesn't move when you change hand positions.

In the standing position, use a strap and brace the bass against your body in the same way.

Tuning the Bass

Electric Tuner

The most common way to tune your bass is with either an electronic tuner or a tuning app for your phone. Luckily, most of these work the same way. Play the 1st string (G) and you may see a G show up on the screen. If the note is too low or flat, you might see an F or F♯. You will need to tighten your string a little until you see the G show up in the middle. If the note played by your 3rd string is too high, you may see A♭ or A. This means you need to loosen your string a little until the G shows up..

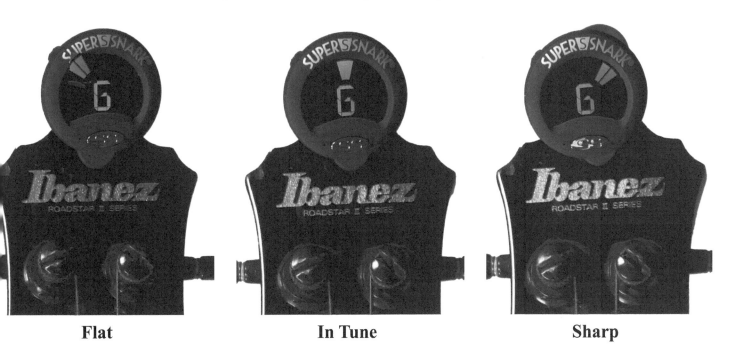

Flat	In Tune	Sharp

Repeat this process for all four strings (E, A, D, G) until they are playing the correct note. It's important that you tune your bass at the start of each practice session. Playing an out of tune bass is like baking a cake with the wrong ingredients. No matter how hard you try, it won't end up tasting very good. Even famous bassists would sound bad if they played an out of tune bass.

Tuning to a Guitar

The four strings of the bass are tuned the same as the four bottom strings on the guitar (E, A, D, G) except that they are tuned an octave lower.

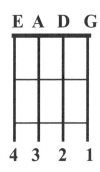

Relative Tuning

Relative tuning means to tune the bass to itself and is used in the following situations:

1. When you don't have an electronic tuner or tuning app to tune from.
2. When you have only one note to tune from.

In the following example, we'll tune all of the strings to the fourth string of the bass which is an E note.

1. Place the ring finger of the left hand behind the 5th fret of the 4th string to produce the 1st note. Tune the 3rd string open (not fretted) until it sounds like the 4th string fretted at the 5th fret.

2. Fret the 3rd string at the 5th fret. Tune the 2nd string open until it sounds like the 3rd string at the 5th fret.

3. Fret the 2nd string at the 5th fret. Tune the 1st string open until it sounds like the 2nd string at the 5th fret.

The following diagram of the bass fret board illustrates the above procedure.

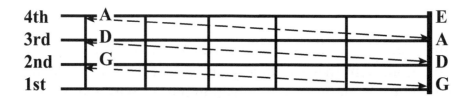

Note - Old dull strings lose their tonal qualities and sometimes tune incorrectly. Check with your teacher or music store to make sure your strings are in good playing condition.

Tablature

This book is written in both tablature and standard music notation. If you wish to learn to read music, consult your local music store for a good book or ask your music teacher. We will explain tablature because of the ease of learning if you are teaching yourself.

Tablature is a system for writing music which shows the proper string and fret to play and which fingers to use.

In bass tablature, the lines represent a string on the bass.

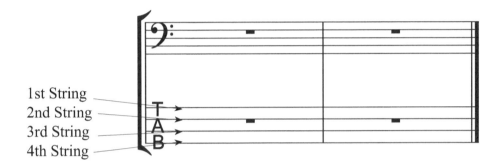

1st String
2nd String
3rd String
4th String

If the string is to be noted, the fret number is written on the appropriate line. Otherwise, a 0 is written. Study the examples below until you understand them thoroughly.

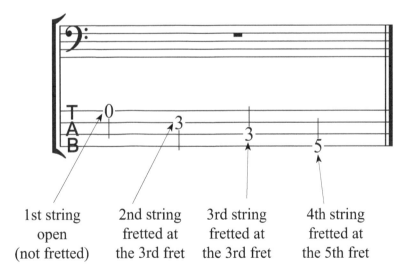

| 1st string open (not fretted) | 2nd string fretted at the 3rd fret | 3rd string fretted at the 3rd fret | 4th string fretted at the 5th fret |

Right Hand Position

In this book, we'll use the first two fingers of the right hand to pick the strings. Some bass players use a pick, but I recommend using fingers because you can get a wider variety of sounds. Using fingers you can sound like you're using a pick, or get a rich, warm sound, or simulate a synthesizer bass, or play with your thumb and get a slap sound. You can also change back and forth between these styles instantly if you're using your fingers.

As mentioned on page 2, the forearm should rest against the top of the bass and brace it against your stomach. The thumb should rest either on the top end of the pickup or on the body of the bass, or on the thumb rest (if your bass has one).

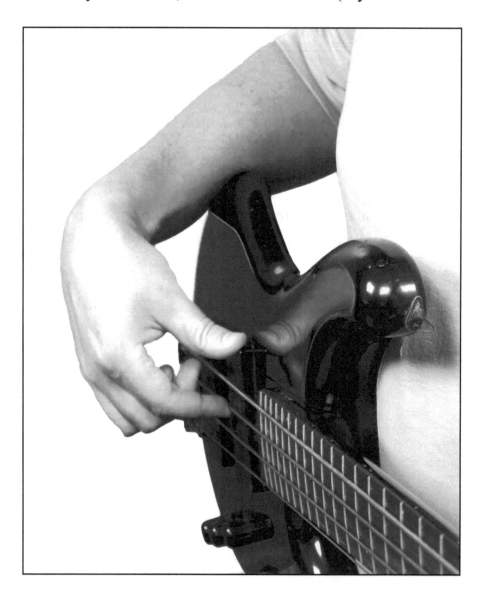

The right wrist should be arched away from the body of the bass.

Use the pads of the first two fingers of the right hand to pluck the strings (don't use your fingertips or fingernails). This is a different technique from finger picking a guitar. Your finger should move directly towards your thumb, not up and away from the bass.

Exercise 1 A

Place the first finger (index) of the right hand on the 3rd string (A) of the bass (I). Use the index finger to pluck the 3rd string. The finger should move towards the thumb and come to rest on the 4th string (E) (II). This is called a rest stroke.

I

II

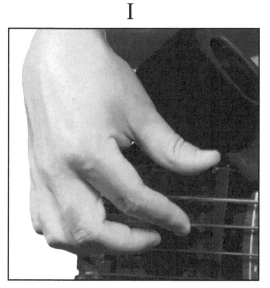 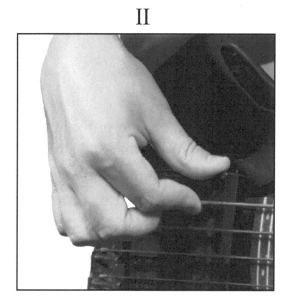

Exercise 1 B

Now do the same thing with your 2nd finger (middle).

I

II

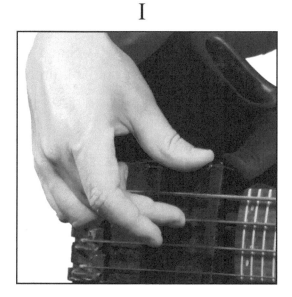 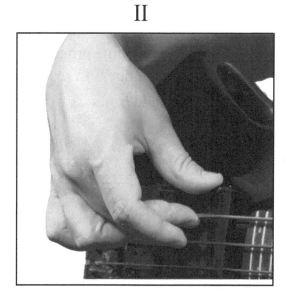

Alternate using the index and middle fingers to pluck the 3rd string (A).

Exercise 2

Follow the same procedure and pick notes on the 2nd string (D). Your fingers should come to rest on the 3rd string (A).

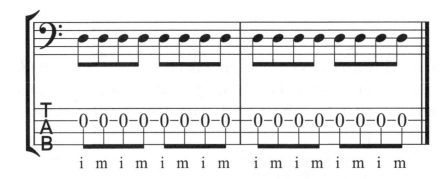

Exercise 3

Using the same procedure, pick notes on the 1st string (G) with your fingers coming to rest on the 2nd string (D).

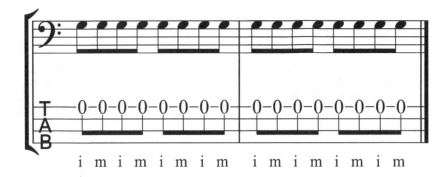

Exercise 4

Again use the same procedure and pick notes on the 4th string (E). Since there is no string for the fingers to rest against, they should come to rest on the thumb. (See diagram next page).

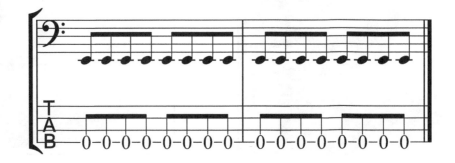

The index finger rests on the thumb after playing the fourth string. See Exercise 4, page 8.

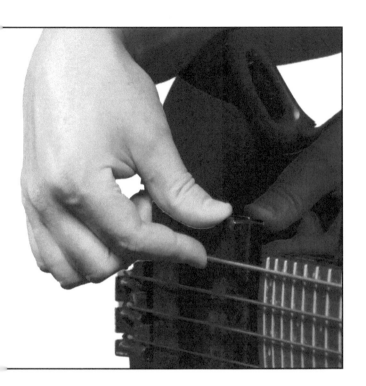 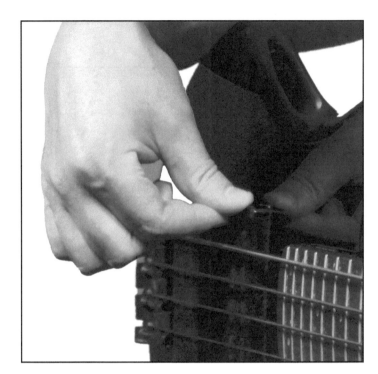

Note - Guard against picking the strings too hard. This is a natural tendency for a beginner, but it can cause buzzes or rattles. Use a smooth motion with the right hand and simply turn up the amp if you need more volume. Do not practice without an amp. Always plug in so that you can hear and develop the proper feel with your right hand.

Left Hand Position

When playing, the position of the left thumb on the back of the neck is very important because it is used to brace and balance the left hand. The pad of the thumb makes contact with the bass neck, as you can see in the following diagrams:

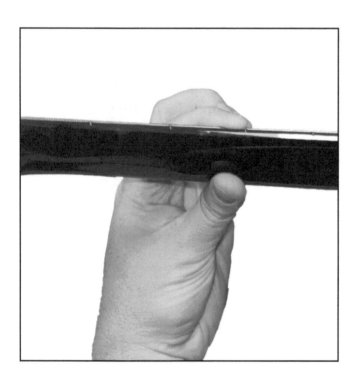
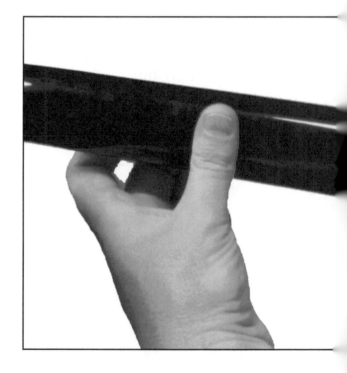

Our First Notes

We will now use the left hand to fret notes on the bass. We'll start with notes in the Key of G since this is a common key for all types of music.

The thumb should be directly underneath the 3rd fret of the bass. This will enable you to play all of the common notes in G without moving your left hand position.

Exercise 5

Press down the pad of the 1st finger of your left hand directly behind the 3rd fret of the 4th string (E) to produce a G note. Pluck the 4th string with the index finger of your right hand.

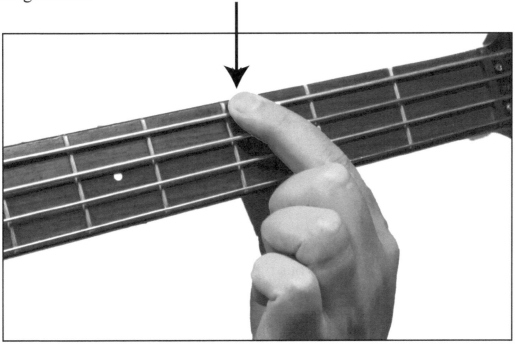

Note that you don't use your fingertips of your left hand as on other stringed instruments. This is for a couple of reasons:

1. Because of the large diameter of bass strings, it is easier to fret the proper note and not slip off of it.

2. You'll eventually start deadening the adjacent strings so that you don't get 2 or more notes ringing at once and causing overtones. This is easier to do using the pads of your fingers.

Exercise 6

Without changing your left hand position from Exercise 5, place the pad of your 1st finger directly behind the 3rd fret of the 3rd string (A) to produce a C note. Pluck the 3rd string with the index finger of your right hand.

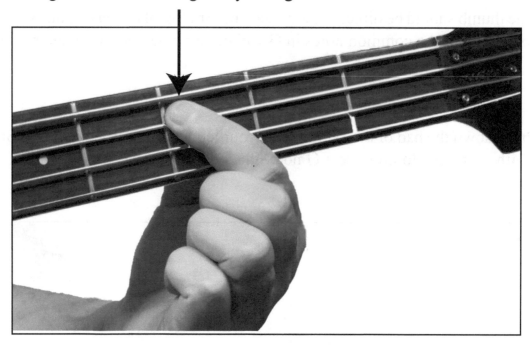

Exercise 7

With the same left hand position, place the pad of your 3rd finger of your left hand directly behind the 5th fret of the 3rd string (A) to produce a D note. Pluck the 3rd string with the index finger of your right hand.

Exercise 8

The whole sequence looks like this in tablature:

The numbers in parenthesis indicate left hand fingering. The letters below the tablature indicate the right hand fingering (i = index, m = middle).

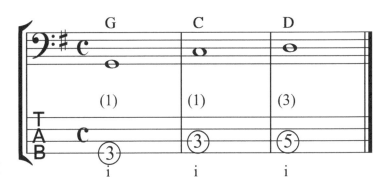

Exercise 9

This exercise uses half notes, which get 2 beats each.

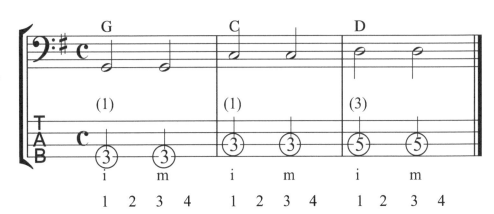

Exercise 10

This exercise uses quarter notes, which get 1 beat each.

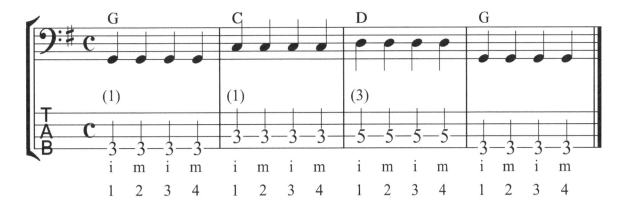

Alternate the fingers of the right hand. Use the index finger on counts 1 & 3 and the middle finger on counts 2 & 4.

OUR FIRST SONG

We'll play all quarter notes to a very common chord progression. Practice the following along with the Audio Tracks.

Getting Started

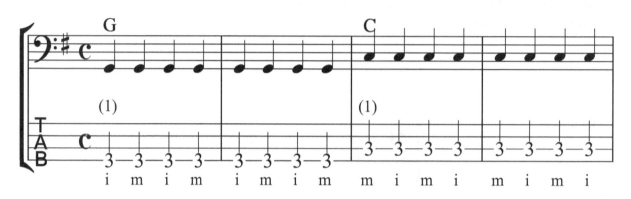

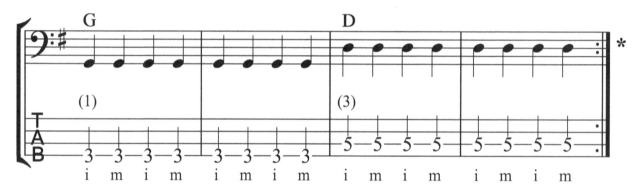

* The repeat signs mean to play the measures between them again. In the exercises and songs in this book, keep repeating them until you feel comfortable and are producing clear, distinct notes.

Buzzing, Muffled, or Unclear Notes

If you aren't getting a clear, distinct sound when playing, check for the following problem areas:
1. Not pressing firmly enough with the left hand. Press the strings firmly, but not so hard as to be painful.
2. Fingers too far from the fret wires or on top of the frets. The fingers of the left hand should be directly behind the fret wires. Check the diagrams in Exercises 5, 6, and 7.

Alternating Bass Notes

It is common in many types of music to alternate the bass note used on each chord. In this case we'll be playing the 1st and 5th notes of each chord. Pay close attention to the right hand fingering.

Exercise 11

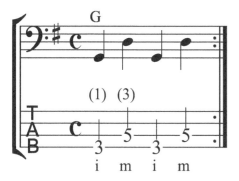

Exercise 12

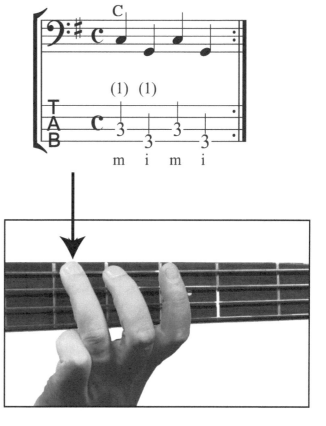

Exercise 13

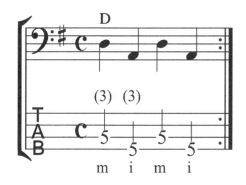

Notice that we've added a new note in Exercise 13. Use the 3rd finger of the left hand to fret the 4th string at the 5th fret to produce the A note.

Anticipation

When you lift your left hand fingers off of the strings, you only need to move about 1/4 inch. Don't move 2 to 3 inches out of position. You should keep them right above the strings so that you are ready to play the next note. This is called anticipation (anticipating the next note). Eliminate the excess finger movement because this only slows you down.

15

We'll now combine Exercises 11, 12, and 13 into a song. The songs that we use in this book are generic chord progressions that would fit several different tunes. Listen to Song 2 on the Audio Tracks, **Good Hearted Woman** by **Waylon Jennings,** to play the following progression.

Alternating Bass

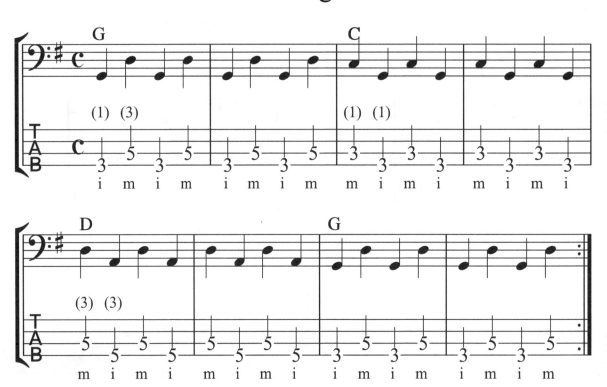

Note - We'll refer to chords quite a bit. A chord is 3 or more notes played simultaneously, usually on a guitar or keyboard. The bass doesn't play chords. You play individual notes on the bass that correspond to the chords that other instruments are playing. The large letters on the tablature denote chords.

In most of this book, we'll be using major chords. A major chord consists of the 1st, 3rd, and 5th notes of that particular scale (example: G chord = G, B, & D, C Chord = C, E, & G, D chord = D, F#, & A). In this song we're playing the 1st and 5th notes of each chord. Refer to the scale chart on page 46.

Note - Each chord progression that we use will fit several popular songs. This is demonstrated on the Audio Tracks. Also note that there are separate track numbers for the slow & fast versions of each song.

Eighth Notes

Eighth notes get 1/2 beat each and are played twice as fast as quarter notes. We'll use the same basic hand position as on the previous songs, but we'll shift up to the 5th fret so that we'll be in the Key of A. Alternate the fingers on the right hand.

Exercise 14

Since eighth notes get a half beat each and there are 4 beats per measure, you would count the notes 1 & 2 & 3 & 4 &, giving each note the same amount of time.

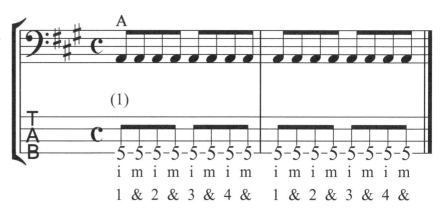

Exercise 15

Using the same technique, we'll play the notes in the D chord.

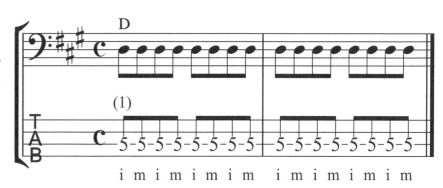

Exercise 16

Now for the notes in the E chord.

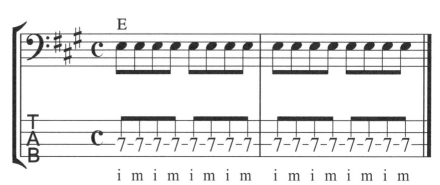

17

Many different songs are played using eighth notes. Listen to Song 3 on the Audio Tracks to play along to **Old Time Rock & Roll** by **Bob Seeger.**

Rocking Eighths

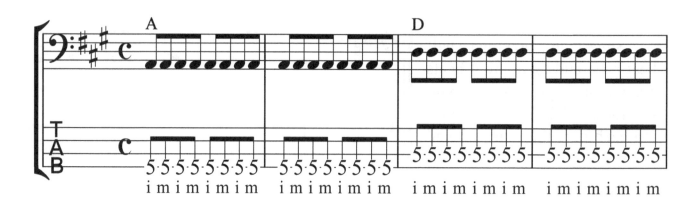

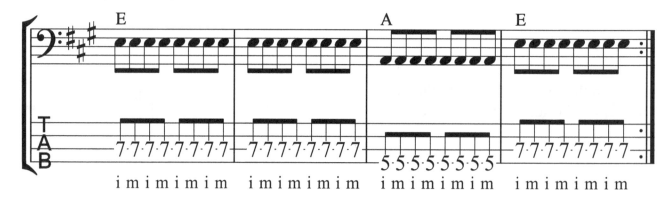

Rock Shuffles

A very common technique uses syncopated eighth notes to produce a rhythm called a rock shuffle. You'll have to listen to the Audio Tracks to get the feel for this rhythm pattern. Notice that this rhythm is written with dotted eighth notes and sixteenth notes.

Exercise 17

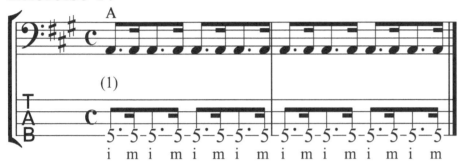

Exercise 18

Use the same technique for the D, E, & B notes.

Exercise 19

Exercise 20

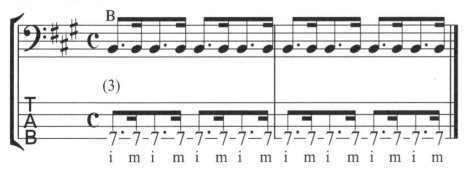

We'll use these exercises to play a common chord pattern in the Key of A. Listen to Song 4 on the Audio Tracks, **That'll Be The Day** by **Buddy Holly.**

Rock Shuffle In A

We're going to use the same rhythm with the right hand, but shift to the key of D. Notice that we're using different left hand fingering to play the notes in D. Listen to Song 5 on the Audio Tracks, **The Wanderer** by **Dion.**

Rock Shuffle In D

Two Beat Rhythm

A common pattern for slow to medium tempo songs uses alternating bass notes and dotted quarter notes, which get 1 1/2 beats. This is called a two beat rhythm. Listen to the Audio Tracks to get the feel of the rhythm.

Exercise 21

Play close attention to the right hand fingering.

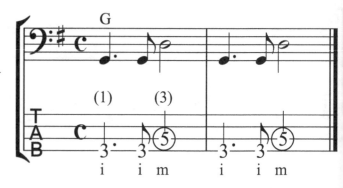

Exercise 22

Same left hand position, but starting on the 3rd string. Play the alternate bass note (G) with the 3rd finger on the 2nd string, 5th fret.

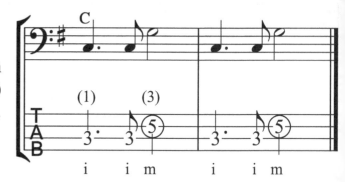

Exercise 23

Now move up to the 5th fret on the 3rd string.

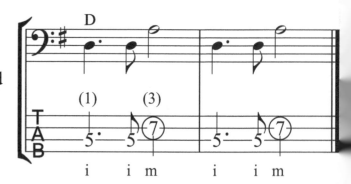

Exercise 24

Go to the 5th fret on the 4th string.

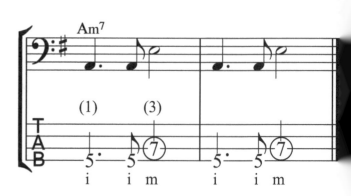

Listen to Song 6 on the Audio Tracks to play **Peaceful, Easy Feeling** by **The Eagles.**

Two Beat In G

Author's Note

It's time to stop and take quick inventory of where we are. You should have accomplished the following:

1. Know the basic positions for the G, C, D, and A notes as well as E and B and be able to play 5 songs from memory.
2. Be comfortable using the right index and middle fingers.
3. Be comfortable playing rhythm patterns using alternating bass, eighth notes, shuffle patterns, and two beat patterns.

Review each of the above to be sure you fully understand them. If you have any questions, consult your teacher or the Audio Tracks. Now read the practice notes and then proceed to the next section.

Practice

The most important part of learning to play the bass is to develop consistent and efficient practice habits. The beginning student must have patience because playing the bass requires training the hands to do movements they have never done before and to strengthen muscles not normally used. You should average 30 minutes of practice each day. With consistent practice you should be comfortable with the bass and be able to play a few songs within a couple of weeks. Once you learn to play a few things on the bass, you'll find the learning process comes easier and your progress will start to snowball.

Following are some helpful hints and pointers concerning practice:

1. Go over your lesson assignment EVERY day. On days that it seems impossible to practice, make yourself go over the lesson for 4 or 5 minutes to reinforce things.
2. Practice 30 minutes a day if you are a beginner and 45 minutes if you are an intermediate. Divide this time into 15 or 20 minute segments. It has been proven that the human mind cannot concentrate heavily for more than 15 minutes.
3. Set up practice times to coincide with other activities such as when you wake up, when you go to bed, or when you come home at the end of the day. 15 minutes in the morning and 15 minutes at night works well for many people.
4. If possible, set up a special practice area. Buy an inexpensive music stand and keep your lessons on it so you can start to work immediately with each practice session.
5. Avoid marathon 2 or 3 hour practice sessions on the weekends. The mind can only concentrate for short periods and most marathon sessions accomplish about the same amount of learning as a 15 minute practice session. In addition, many students use the "Marathon Practice Session" as an excuse to not practice every day.
6. Learn to identify and focus on the hard parts of each song. Put your efforts there as opposed to playing a song from start to finish over and over. Some techniques and movements require several hundred repetitions over several weeks while others are learned immediately after an few tries.
7. Practice the bass at first by looking in a mirror to make sure you are using the proper position.
8. Relax - if frustrated with a particular measure or technique, go to another or just take a break and come back after you feel better.
9. Ask your teacher or a friend to let you know how you are doing every couple of weeks. It is very encouraging because they notice your progress even though you think you are standing still.
10. Record and listen to your own playing. This will help you locate areas that need work and also measure progress. Your tapes will improve as you practice more and more.
11. Remember always - Bass playing is a lot of fun no matter what your level of competence. Relax and enjoy yourself.

Section 2

Playing

For Audio Access, go to this internet address:

cvls.com/extras/begbass

Walking Bass Lines

A very common bass pattern, called walking bass, uses quarter notes and moves about on the fret board quite a bit. We'll be in the Key of A and play walking patterns for the A, D, and E chords.

Exercise 25

We'll move down the bass neck for these notes and start with the A chord.

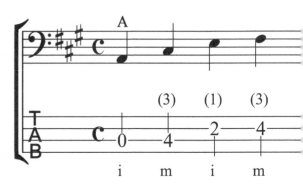

1st Note

Pick the 3rd string (A) open with the right index finger.

2nd Note

Place the 3rd finger of the left hand on the 3rd string at the 4th fret. Pluck the string with the right middle finger.

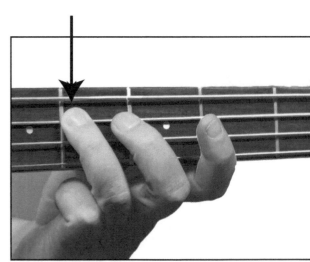

3rd Note

Place the 1st finger of your left hand on the 2nd string (D) at the 2nd fret. Pluck the 2nd string with the right index finger.

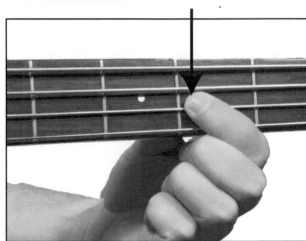

26

4th Note

Place the 3rd finger of your left hand on the 2nd string (D) at the 4th fret. Pluck the 2nd string with the right middle finger.

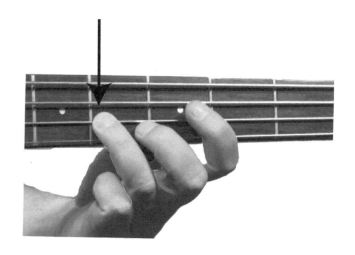

Now play these 4 notes over and over until you are comfortable with them.

Exercise 26

This is the same left hand pattern, but we'll start on the 2nd string (D).

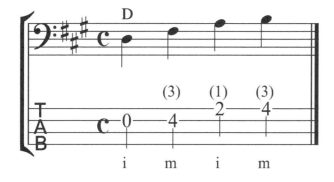

Exercise 27

Again the same left hand pattern, but starting on the 4th string (E).

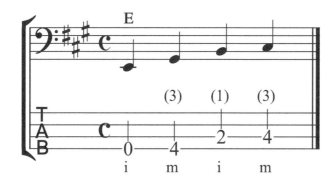

We'll now use these patterns with a very common chord progression called 12 Bar Blues (there are 12 bars or measures, hence the name). Listen to Song 7 on the Audio Tracks to play along to **Johnny B. Goode** by **Chuck Berry.**

12 Bar Blues In A

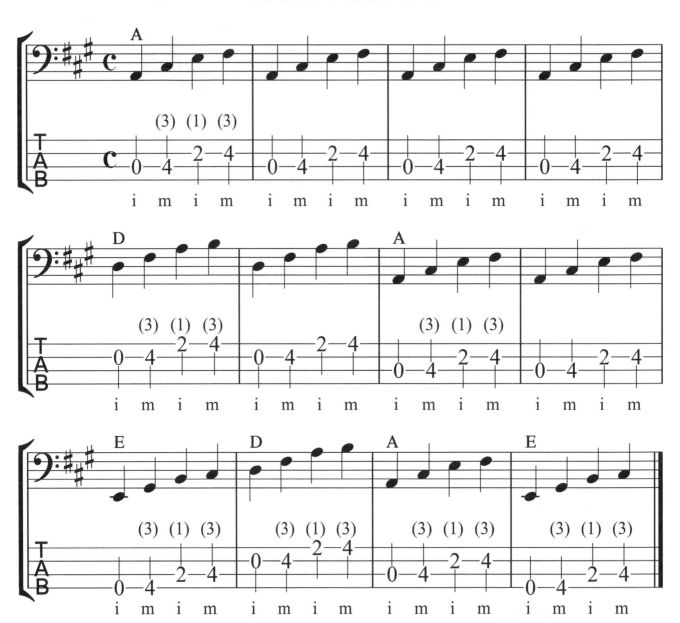

Note that we are playing the 1st, 3rd, 5th, and 6th notes of the scale for each chord (A chord = A, C♯, E, F♯, D chord = D, F♯, A, B, E chord = E, G♯, B, C♯). Refer to the scale chart on page 46.

Practice the following two patterns for the B chord.

Exercise 28 A

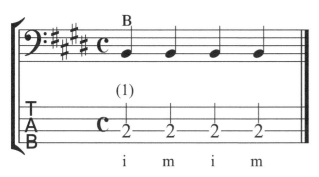

Exercise 28 B

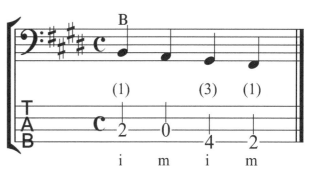

We'll use the E, A, and B patterns to play a slightly different 12 Bar Blues in the Key of E.

12 Bar Blues In E

Walking Eighth Notes

Exercise 29

It is also very common to use eighth notes in a walking pattern.

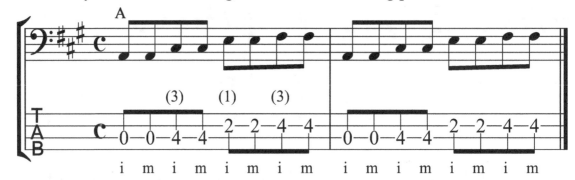

We'll now use this pattern for the 12 Bar Blues in A. Notice the last measure.

Walking Eighths In A

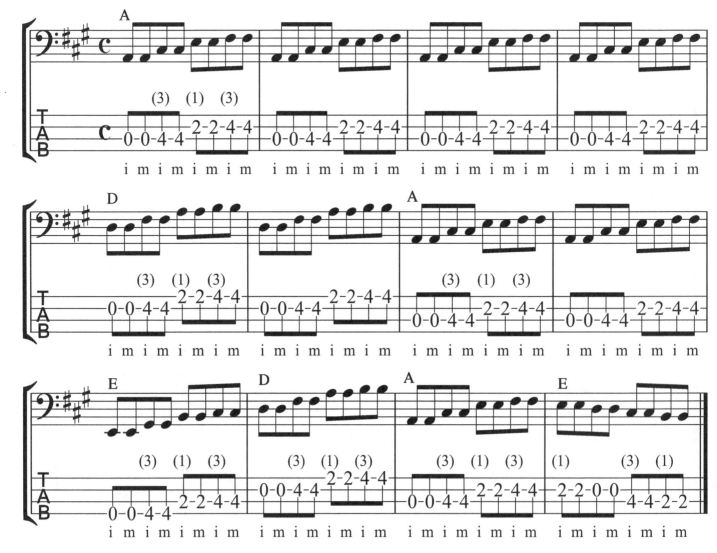

Walking Shuffle

Back to the Key of E and the syncopated rhythm we used on pages 19 - 21.
We'll also use variations on the left hand pattern.

Exercise 30 A

Exercise 30 B

Listen to Song 10 on the Audio Tracks to play along to **Kansas City**.

Walking Shuffle In E

Scales

Playing scales on a bass is great exercise for stretching your fingers. We'll start with an A scale, since we've been playing in the Key of A quite a bit. Make sure to use the correct fingers.

Exercise 31

Note that we start and end on the root note (A).

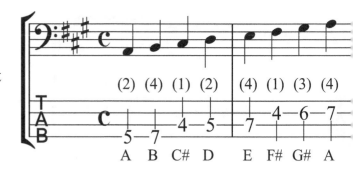

Exercise 32

Now play the reverse starting with the high A or octave.

Practicing scales is a great way to warm up and get the fingers really going. Start every practice session by playing scales to get the maximum use of your practice time.

This pattern will work for any scale whose root note is on the 4th string. Simply place your 2nd finger on the appropriate note and use the exact same finger pattern.

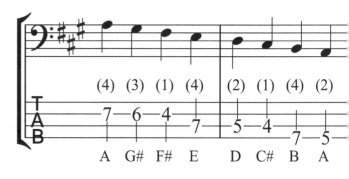

Exercise 33

Play a G scale as shown below.

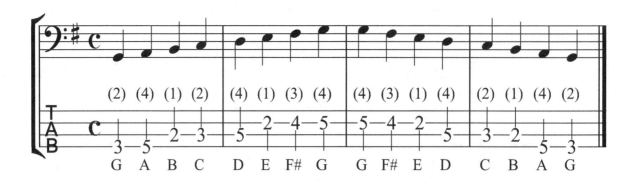

Scale Chart

Consult the following chart to find the starting point for other scales whose root note is on the 4th string.

Key	Fret
F	1
F♯ or G♭	2
G	3
G♯ or A♭	4
A	5
A♯ or B♭	6
B	7
C	8

D Scale

The following scale pattern is the same as the A scale, just start on the D note.

Exercise 34

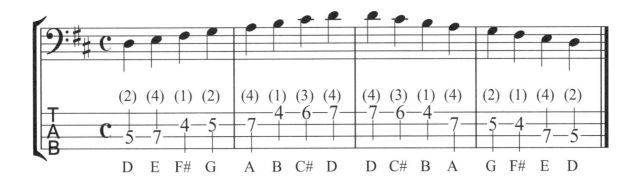

This pattern will work for any scale whose root note is on the 3rd string. Simply place your 2nd finger on the appropriate note and use the same finger pattern.

Exercise 35

Play a C scale as shown below.

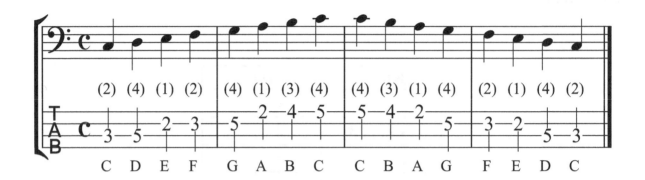

Consult the following chart to find the starting point for other scales whose root note is on the 3rd string.

Key	Fret
A# of B♭	1
B	2
C	3
C# or D♭	4
D	5
D# or E♭	6
E	7
F	8

Consult the Appendix on pages 45 - 47 for more discussion.

Up the Neck Walks

Walking bass patterns like we practiced earlier in the book can be played up the neck. They will be based on the scales we just worked on. We'll start in the Key of A, so review the A scale.

Exercise 36

The first four notes are the same A pattern notes that we played on pages 26 - 28, but they are played in a different position on the bass neck. We are adding four notes to make this a two measure pattern.

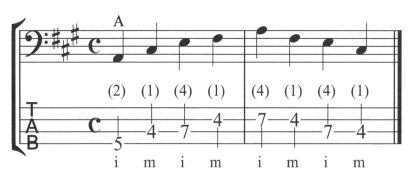

Exercise 37

Use the same left hand position for D and start on the 3rd string 5th fret.

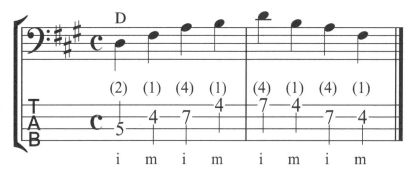

Exercise 38

Shift the 2nd finger up to the 7th fret of the 3rd string for the E pattern.

Make sure to use the correct finger to fret each note.

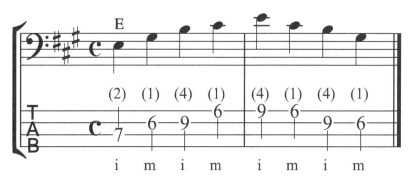

Using these three patterns, we'll play a common walking pattern up the neck.
Note that the last measure of the song is also different.

Walking Up the neck

Bass Runs

A good way to apply the scale pattern is to connect chord patterns with bass runs. Using a basic pattern similar to the one on page 16, we'll link the chord patterns together with bass runs. This is in the Key of G, so review the G scale.

Exercise 39

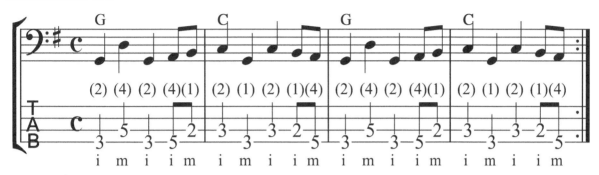

Exercise 40

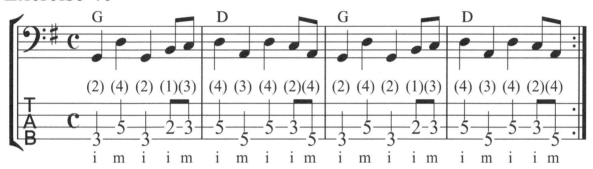

Bass Runs In G

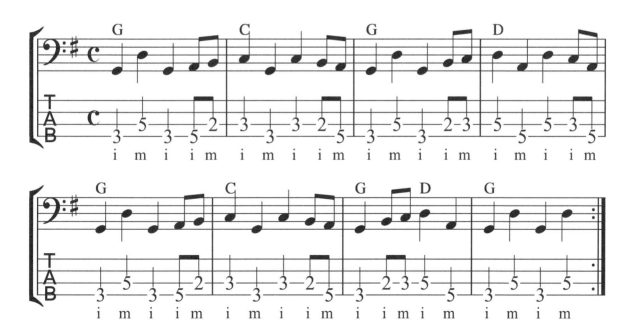

We'll now plug bass runs into the two beat rhythm we used on page 23. This will be in the Key of G, starting at the high G and coming back down. Pay close attention to the fingering.

Walking Two Beat

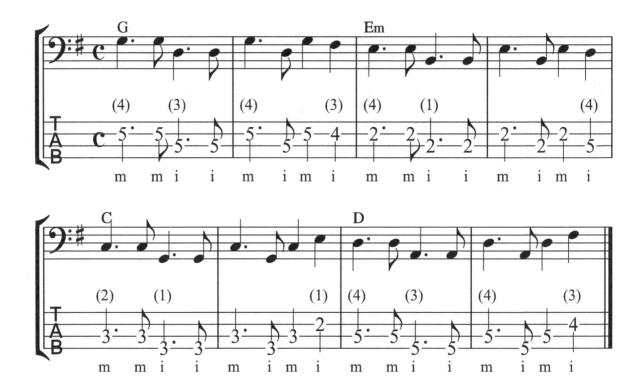

By combining the two beat rhythm and finger patterns used on up the neck walks, we can come up with a very common pattern used for slow rock tunes.

Exercise 41

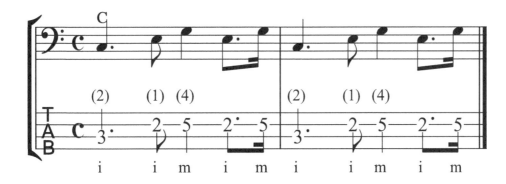

Notice the triplets in the last two measures. These are 3 notes played in the space of 2. Listen to the Audio Tracks for the rhythm.

Slow Rock

Dampened Eighth Notes

A common technique among modern bass players is to dampen the string with the little finger of the right hand. This is done to get a sharper, more distinct sound. This will simulate the sound of a synthesizer bass or playing with a pick and dampening with the heel of the hand.

Exercise 42

Place the little finger of the right hand on the 4th string. Pick the 4th string with the index finger. Press down firmly enough with the little finger to get a dampened sound.

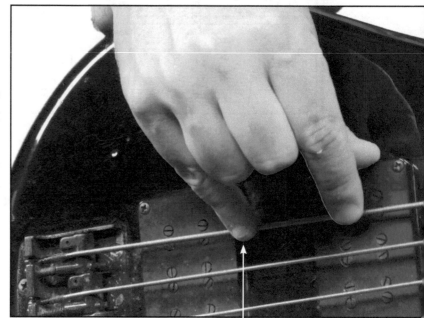

The dot above or below the note means staccato. On bass tablature, use the dampening technique when you see staccato marks.

Exercise 43

Turn back to pages 18, 20, & 21 and play these three songs using the dampening technique.

Rock Riffs

Here's a finger pattern that's very common in rock music. Listen to Song 16 on the Audio Tracks to play along to **Addicted To Love** by **Robert Palmer.**

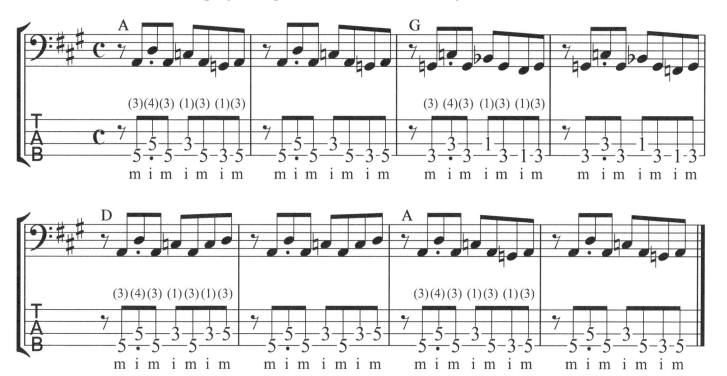

Here's a variation. Listen to Song 17 to play along to **Billy Jean** by **Michael Jackson.**

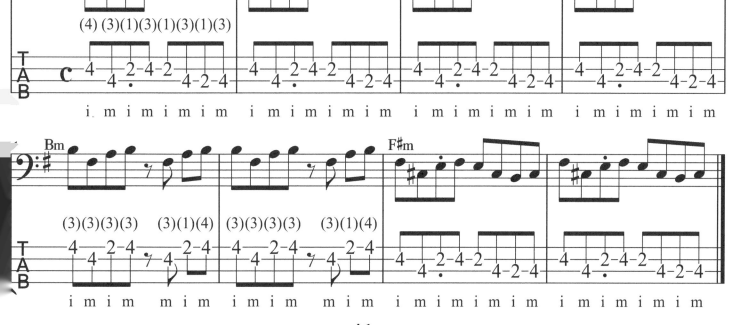

Here's another variation on the finger pattern. Listen to Song 18 on the Audio Tracks to play along to **Under My Thumb** by **The Rolling Stones.**

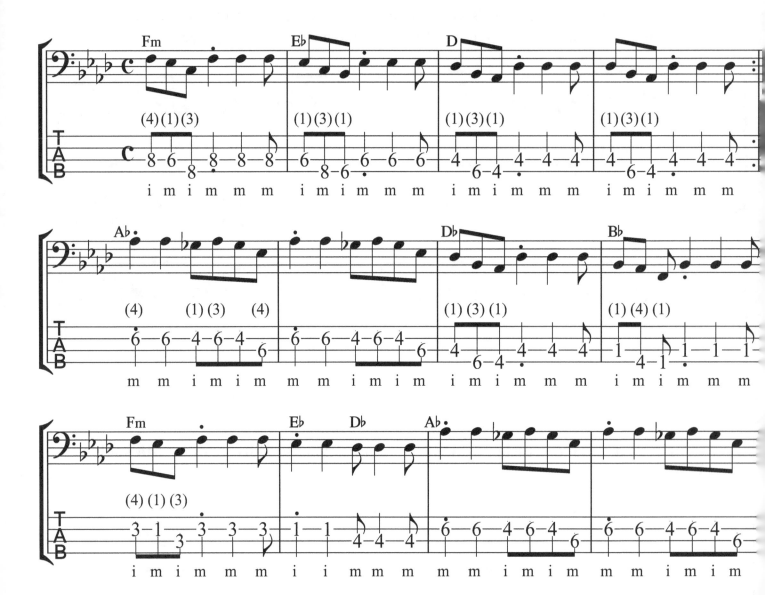

For the E♭ and D♭, place the 1st finger across the 3rd and 4th strings to play the notes indicated so that you don't have to move your fingers as much. When you see a single staccato mark, cut that note off by releasing the pressure with the left hand. Don't pick the finger up off of the string, just release the pressure.

Other Patterns

Here's a real finger stretcher that's used in several popular tunes. Listen to Song 19 on the Audio Tracks to play **La Bamba** by **Richie Valens.**

Exercise 44

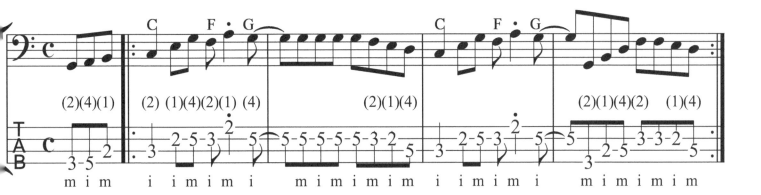

Exercise 45

Here's a common Motown bass line.

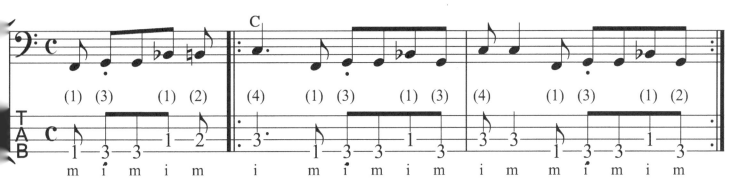

Walking Variations

There are several variations on the walking bass patterns that we used earlier.

Exercise 46

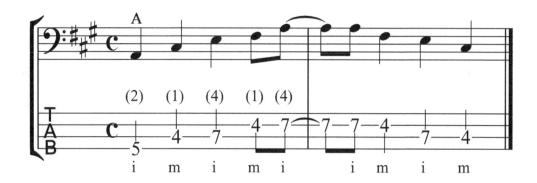

Exercise 47

This is a bluesy walk. We'll add the ♭7th of the scale to get the bluesy sound.

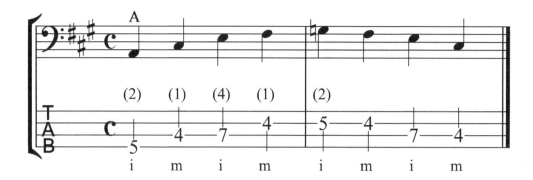

Exercise 48

This would typically be used in a fast rock song. Noticed the hammer-on in this example.

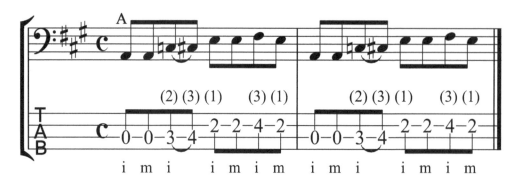

Appendix

For Audio Access, go to this internet address:

cvls.com/extras/begbass

Summary

This book is intended to give you a broad understanding of the bass and a basis for many different styles that can be played. You should now work on expanding your repertoire by working through other books, playing along with CD's, and playing with other musicians.

If you stop and thumb back through the techniques we've covered in this book, it becomes apparent that a lot of bass playing involves playing out of certain finger positions or patterns. I'll attempt to explain this so that you can get a better overview of what you're actually doing on the fret board. When we play the scales as on pages 32 - 34, you can see that there are 7 notes in a major scale.

Notes In Major Scales

Scale		1	2	3	4	5	6	7
Key of C		C	D	E	F	G	A	B
Key of G	(1♯)	G	A	B	C	D	E	F♯
Key of D	(2♯)	D	E	F♯	G	A	B	C♯
Key of A	(3♯)	A	B	C♯	D	E	F♯	G♯
Key of E	(4♯)	E	F♯	G♯	A	B	C♯	D♯
Key of F	(1♭)	F	G	A	B♭	C	D	E
Key of B♭	(2♭)	B♭	C	D	E♭	F	G	A
Key of E♭	(3♭)	E♭	F	G	A♭	B♭	C	D
Key of A♭	(4♭)	A♭	B♭	C	D♭	E♭	F	G

We have been referring to the notes and the corresponding chords by their letter names (A, D, E). We'll now start referring to them by their number. The majority of songs in this book are three chord songs, with the chords being the 1st, 4th, and 5th notes in each key. Refer to the following chart.

Common Chords			Commonly Called	Example
1st	1st note of scale (major chord)		(Tonic)	G
4th	4th note of scale (major chord)		(Subdominant)	C
5th	5th note of scale (major chord)		(Dominant)	D
6th minor	6th note of scale (minor chord)		(Relative Minor)	Em
2nd	2nd note of scale (major chord)			A
2nd minor	2nd note of scale (minor chord)			Am
3rd	3rd note of scale (major chord)			B
3rd minor	3rd note of scale (minor chord)			Bm
♭7th	7th note of scale moved down a half step (major chord)			F
1 (7th)	1st note of scale (dominant 7th chord) 1→ 1 (7th) → 4			G⁷
5 (7th)	5th note of scale (dominant 7th chord) 5→ 5 (7th)→ 1			D⁷
♭3rd	3rd note of scale moved down a half step (major chord)			B♭
♭6th	6th note of scale moved down a half step (major chord)			E♭

Most of the songs up through page 37 are 3 chord songs with the chords being the 1st, 4th, and 5th chords in each key. On the bass, we play a single note or series of notes that correspond to the chord changes. For example, on page 36 we're in the Key of A using A, D, and E chords (1, 4, 5). We play a walking pattern that uses the same relative finger positions for each chord, just a different starting point depending on which chord we're playing. The A chord pattern starts on an A note, the D pattern starts on a D note, and the E pattern starts on an E note.

On page 39, we take this even further. In the Key of C, we're using the same finger pattern for the C, D, E, and F chords (1, 2, 3, & 4). On each chord we start with the root note of that chord (C note for the C chord) and use the exact same finger pattern for each one.

Here is some information on what notes compose each chord.

Chord	Notes	Example	
Major	1st, 3rd, 5th	G	G, B, D
7th	1st, 3rd, 5th, $\flat$7th	G^7	G, B, D, F
Minor	1st, $\flat$3rd, 5th	Gm	G, B$\flat$, D
Minor 7th	1st, $\flat$3rd, 5th, $\flat$7th	Gm^7	G, B$\flat$, D, F
Major 7th	1st, 3rd, 5th, 7th	$Gmaj^7$	G, B, D, F$\sharp$
9th	1st, 2nd, 3rd, 5th, $\flat$7th	G^9	G, A, B, D, F
sus^4	1st, 3rd, 4th, 5th	$Gsus^4$	G, B, C, D
Diminished	1st, $\flat$3rd, $\flat$5th	Gdim	G, B$\flat$, D$\flat$
Augmented	1st, 3rd, $\sharp$5th	G+	G, B, D$\sharp$

Conclusion

As you gain a feel for the notes and different patterns on the bass, keep in mind the role that the bass plays in a band. The bass, along with the kick drum, provides the down beat of the music. You should provide a very solid bottom end to the music. Many bass players have a tendency to overplay and, as a result, muddle the music.

As you develop bass lines for songs, always keep the principle of simplicity in mind. When in doubt, underplay. Leave the lead lines to the guitar or keyboard and concentrate on emphasizing the down beat.

As you study many styles, you'll find that many of the most respected and most famous bass players play fairly simple bass lines. They understand their role in the music that is being played. Don't become a frustrated guitar player who ends up on bass. Develop the proper attitude of a bass player and you'll enjoy playing music more and the musicians you play with will also enjoy it more.

Circle of 5ths

The circle of 5ths is useful for memorizing the order of sharp or flat keys, as well as the order in which the sharps or flats occur.

Beginning with the key of C and moving clockwise in steps of 5ths, each key has one more sharp than the one before it. Moving counterclockwise from C in steps of 4ths, each key has one more flat than the one before it.

Each new sharp is the 7th of the key in which it occurs. Each new flat is the 4th of the key in which it occurs.

The key signatures as they would appear in music notation are shown inside the circle. To figure out the name of the flat keys from the key signature, use the next to last flat. Move the last sharp up one note (1/2 step or 1 fret) to figure out the name of the sharp keys.

Notice that there are 12 different major keys, but three of them have different names. Keys that have the same key signature, but have different names are called Enharmonic keys.

The relative minor key of each major key, which is the 6th of that key, is shown inside the circle. The relative minor has the same key signature as its relative major key.

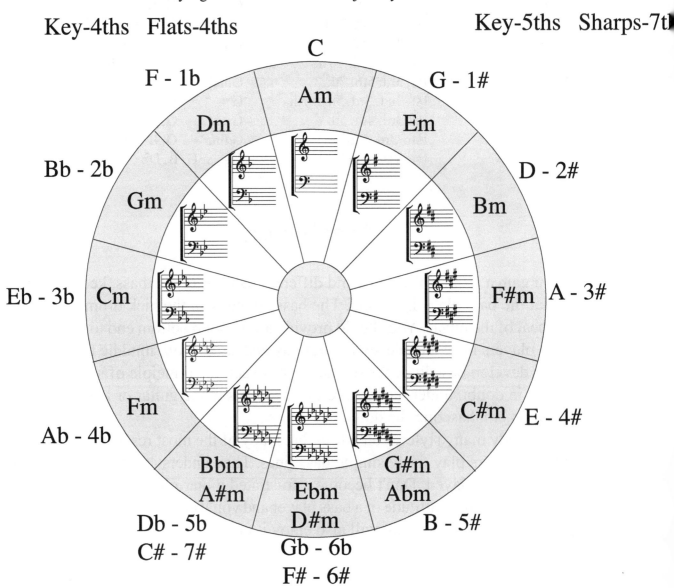

48

Follow-up Bass Course

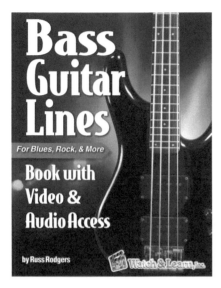

    Bass Guitar Lines Book with Online Video & Audio Access by Russ Rodgers will teach you how to play forty different intermediate level bass lines. This course covers a variety of techniques, tempos, and different styles of music like Blues, Rock, R&B, and Reggae. Learning these lines will let you get comfortable playing a wider range of ideas around the fretboard and provide effective practice material. The online access includes audio tracks and over eight hours of video instruction showing each bass line explained note-by-note with fingerings and rhythmic count. It is then played along with a rhythm track at three different speeds (slow, medium, and fast). All of the music notation is included in this book along with bass tablature for each line. Increase your repertoire and versatility by learning multiple variations of standard bass lines.

    This book is available on Amazon.com.

Made in United States
Troutdale, OR
11/02/2023